M000106741

FOUNDER OF
SIMPLISTICALLY LIVING

Adorkable
Bubble Bath
Crafts

50 EASY, GEEKY-CLEAN CRAFTS TO MAKE KIDS' BATH TIME AWESOME

PAGE STREET
PUBLISHING CO.

PAGE STREET
PUBLISHING CO.

Copyright © 2017 Brittanie Pyper

First published in 2017 by

Page Street Publishing Co.

27 Congress Street, Suite 105

Salem, MA 01970

www.pagestreetpublishing.com

All rights reserved. No part of this book may be reproduced or used, in any form or by any means, electronic or mechanical, without prior permission in writing from the publisher.

Distributed by Macmillan, sales in Canada by The Canadian Manda Group.

21   20   19   18   17   1   2   3   4   5

ISBN-13: 9781624143755

ISBN-10: 162414375X

Library of Congress Control Number: 2017930307

Cover and book design by Page Street Publishing Co.

Photography by Brittanie Pyper

Printed and bound in the United States

As a member of 1% for the Planet, Page Street Publishing protects our planet by donating to nonprofits like The Trustees, which focuses on local land conservation. Learn more at onepercentfortheplanet.org.

DEDICATION

To my boys, Kayzen and Tarek: May you always remember the times we shared chasing zombies or pretending to fight crime. I love you both more than the turtles love pizza (and that's a lot). You are the future nerds of the world and don't ever be afraid to let that creativity shine!

CONTENTS

Creative Coloring

Bedtime Readiness

After Bath Care

Introduction

To a child (big or small), a bathtub is never just a bathtub. Whether it becomes a boat, a plane or even a pirate ship, bath time is fun.

It's a time when kids of all ages can unwind and let their imagination go wild all while getting squeaky clean. As a mom, nothing makes me happier than knowing my kids are happy and exploring the true meaning of what it's like to be a kid.

That is why I encourage more play and fun in our home. Whether it's crafting up a wicked potion or fighting off a horde of zombies, we do it together. That is what this book is all about—bringing out the kid in us all and making epic homemade bath products that everyone will enjoy.

These will not only enhance the imagination, but they will make bath time bubbles of fun! So let's get crafting!

Safety First

Before we can start popping bubbles, there a few safety procedures that are worth noting. Without these, the crafts may end in a disaster. It's like playing Monopoly without the play money. It's not fun and nobody wins! So, here are a few safety tips to keep in mind while making these wonderfully crafted bath products. After all we want more play time, right?

1. Always supervise children during craft time. Some of these crafts require the use of heat, chemicals or sprays that can become harmful if not handled properly.

2. Use proper hand mitts and safe handling when dealing with hot products.

3. Read all labels and know the supplies you are working with.

4. Some of the crafts in this book use small toys that can be a choking hazard for children three and under.

5. Keep oils and other chemicals out of reach of little ones and pets as they may become sick if ingested.

6. Always use skin-safe essential oils and fragrance oils. Oils found near candles and candle making products are not skin-safe and can cause burning if used. An oil must read "skin-safe" in order to be used in these crafts.

7. Ensure all containers that are going to be microwaved are microwave-safe prior to use.

8. Be aware of any products that may be an allergen for your child.

9. Designate any containers and utensils used for these crafts, "for crafts only." You cannot use the containers and/or utensils for any food use once they have been used for bath crafts. An easy way to remember is to use a permanent marker to mark the bottom of your containers/supplies with a "S" that stands for soap. The only exception to this is on products that are made from edible food ingredients.

10. Some crafts in this book involve the use of food coloring. We use a small amount, which should not cause staining. However, be aware that if you use more than the recommended amount you may see slight staining. Always test on a small area before using in your bath and/or shower.

FUN FACTS:

 Throughout this book, you will find that many of the crafts use some of the same ingredients as others. That makes bath crafting even easier because you will likely have everything you need on hand to complete each project!

Supplies in this book can be found at places such as Amazon, Michael's, Hobby Lobby and Wholesale Supplies Plus.

FIZZY FUN

If you've ever had an itch to watch something (safely) explode but haven't taken the plunge, the bath bomb is your friend. Bath bombs are fun to watch because they fizz and dissolve right before your eyes. All it takes is a little bit of magic, some totally safe ingredients and a bit of imagination to make these little fizzies. But watch out! Some of these might bring more than you bargained for!

Alien Experiment 626 Bath Bomb

Experimental testing is usually what causes all sorts of chaos. In this particular case, an adorable little creature makes his way into your home, and while he does cause chaos as he explores an unfamiliar place, don't let that get you down! He's from another planet but packs loveable characteristics you just can't help but adore.

YIELD: 1 bath bomb

MATERIALS

½ cup (145 g) baking soda

¼ cup (57 g) citric acid

¼ cup (57 g) cornstarch

¼ cup (57 g) Epsom salt

1 tbsp (14 g) blue bath bomb powder colorant (to achieve the darker color; if you want a lighter color, you can use food coloring)

1 tbsp (15 ml) castor oil (can also use coconut oil)

1 tbsp (15 ml) water

2–3 drops blueberry fragrance oil (or skin-safe oil of your choosing)

Round plastic bath bomb mold (can use a plastic ornament)

Mini alien figure

White food marker or gel food coloring

DIRECTIONS

1. In a mixing bowl, mix the baking soda, citric acid, cornstarch, Epsom salt and the blue bath bomb powder colorant (dry ingredients).

2. In a separate bowl, mix the castor oil, water and fragrance oil (wet ingredients).

3. Slowly pour the wet ingredients into the dry ingredients with one hand while mixing with the other. Do not pour too fast or you will cause the fizzing reaction. You want your mixture to stick together but not be too wet. Once you can grab a handful and it sort of clumps together like wet sand it is ready. If it's too dry, add a few drops of water.

4. Grab your round plastic mold and start packing one side of the mold with the mixture extremely tight; the tighter, the better. Take your alien figure and stick it into the middle of the mold.

5. Take the other side of your mold and pack more of the mixture in tightly. Then snap the two sides of the mold together and allow this to sit overnight. Once the bath bomb has had time to dry, carefully remove it from the mold.

6. Take your white food marker and write "626" on the front. When ready, just pop it in the bath and watch your little creature make his way into your home!

(continued)

Alien Experiment 626 Bath Bomb (cont.)

Dragon Egg Bath Bomb

You can find all sorts of adorable and unique pets at your local exotic pet store, but you know what you can't find? Dragons! Dragons can only be hatched from the finest eggs found in the finest caves. Don't have a cave around? Don't worry. These bath bombs will be hatching your new little fire-breathing friend in no time.

YIELD: 1 bath bomb

MATERIALS

½ cup (145 g) baking soda

¼ cup (57 g) citric acid

¼ cup (57 g) cornstarch

¼ cup (57 g) Epsom salt

3 tsp (15 ml) castor oil (can also use coconut oil), divided

3 tsp (15 ml) water, divided

6 drops dragon's blood fragrance oil (or skin-safe oil of your choosing)

Lime green food coloring

Green food coloring

Clear plastic egg mold

Mini plastic dragon figure (small enough to fit inside your mold)

DIRECTIONS

1. In a mixing bowl, mix the baking soda, citric acid, cornstarch and Epsom salt (dry ingredients). In a separate bowl, mix 1 teaspoon of castor oil, 1 teaspoon of water, 2 drops of fragrance oil and 2 drops of lime green food coloring (wet ingredients) into each bowl.

2. Next, evenly divide the dry mixture into 3 separate cups or bowls.

3. Begin dyeing each one of these separately with the wet, colored ingredients from the previous step. Slowly pour the wet ingredients into the dry ingredients with one hand while mixing with the other. Do not pour too fast or you will cause the fizzing reaction. You want your mixture to stick together but not be too wet. Once you can grab a handful and it sort of clumps together like wet sand it is ready.

4. Repeat step 3 with the remaining bowls by gradually adding more green food coloring so you will have 3 different shades of green.

5. Take one half of your egg and pack in some of the mixture with one color. Repeat by packing in random amounts of each color to give it a cool colorful effect. Then take a mini dragon figure and stick it into the middle of the mold. Take the other half of the plastic mold and pack in some of the mixture like you did before and snap the mold shut. You can keep the two halves together by using a small piece of duct tape to wrap around the outside.

   Leave the mixture in the plastic egg mold overnight. Once dried, carefully remove the plastic mold. When ready, plop it into the bath and watch your baby dragon hatch from its egg!

(continued)

The Jokester's Laughing Bomb

HAHA—this wicked little bath bomb would make any bat run in fear. It's filled with twisted colors and might just enhance your fears. Don't worry—the City isn't in trouble, but we can't promise your bathtub won't be!

YIELD: 1 bath bomb

MATERIALS

½ cup (145 g) baking soda

¼ cup (57 g) citric acid

¼ cup (57 g) cornstarch

¼ cup (57 g) Epsom salt

1 tbsp (15 ml) castor oil (can also use coconut oil)

1 tbsp (15 ml) water

Essential oil

4 drops neon green food coloring

2 drops green food coloring

Round plastic bath bomb mold (can use a plastic ornament)

Purple food marker or purple gel food coloring

DIRECTIONS

1. In a mixing bowl, mix the baking soda, citric acid, cornstarch and Epsom salt (dry ingredients).

2. In a separate bowl, mix the castor oil, water, essential oil and the green food colorings (wet ingredients).

3. Slowly pour the wet ingredients into the dry ingredients with one hand while mixing with the other. Do not pour too fast or you will cause the fizzing reaction. You want your mixture to stick together but not be too wet. Once you can grab a handful and it sort of clumps together like wet sand it is ready. If it's too dry, add a few drops of water.

4. Grab your round plastic mold and start packing one side of the mold with the mixture extremely tight; the tighter, the better. Complete with the other half of the plastic mold then snap the two sides together.

5. Allow the bath bomb to stay in the mold overnight to dry. Once dry, carefully remove the mold.

6. Take your purple food marker and write "HA HA" all over the bath bomb. Allow the writing to dry then place back into the mold until ready to use.

7. When ready, plop this bath bomb into the bath and watch those crazy laughs fade away!

Monster Egg Bath Bomb

Hey there little egg—while you typically have to incubate eggs for a long period of time before they will hatch, these eggs are a little different. Simply throw them into a tub full of water and watch the little monsters hatch from their eggs in no time! Think of how fast you can truly catch them all!

YIELD: 1 bath bomb

MATERIALS

½ cup (145 g) baking soda

¼ cup (57 g) citric acid

¼ cup (57 g) cornstarch

¼ cup (57 g) Epsom salt

1 tbsp (15 ml) castor oil (can also use coconut oil)

1 tbsp (15 ml) water

2–3 drops lime essential oil (or oil of your choosing)

Clear plastic egg mold

Mini monster plastic figure

Green food marker or green gel food dye

Purple food marker or purple gel food dye

DIRECTIONS

1. In a mixing bowl, mix the baking soda, citric acid, cornstarch and Epsom salt (dry ingredients). In a separate bowl, mix the castor oil, water and essential oil (wet ingredients).

2. Slowly pour the wet ingredients into the dry ingredients with one hand while mixing with the other. Do not pour too fast or you will cause the fizzing reaction. You want your mixture to stick together but not be too wet. Once you can grab a handful and it sort of clumps together like wet sand it is ready. If it's too dry, add a few drops of water.

3. Grab your plastic egg mold and start packing one side of the mold with the mixture extremely tight; the tighter the better.

4. Take your plastic monster figure and stick it into the middle of the mold. Take the other side of your mold and pack more of the mixture in tightly. Then snap the two sides of the egg together and allow this to sit overnight. You can keep the two halves together by using a small piece of duct tape to wrap around the outside.

5. Once your monster egg has had time to dry, carefully separate the two plastic sides of the mold and you will have an entirely white bath bomb egg. Use the green and purple food markers or gel food dye to draw little circles/ovals onto the egg to give it an authentic look.

6. When ready to use, just pop it into the bath and enjoy watching your little monster hatch!

0.5/2km

Spider Sense Bath Bomb

Bathers beware that the tingly, fizzing reaction in this bath bomb might just hatch you some baby spiders. They don't mean you any harm. Instead, they want to help you feel wall-clingingly clean and help take your senses to new heights!

YIELD: 1 bath bomb

MATERIALS

½ cup (145 g) baking soda

¼ cup (57 g) citric acid

¼ cup (57 g) cornstarch

¼ cup (57 g) Epsom salt

1 tbsp (15 ml) castor oil (can also use coconut oil)

1 tbsp (15 ml) water

Essential oil

4–5 drops red food coloring

Round plastic bath bomb mold (can use a plastic ornament)

Spider sprinkles

Black food marker or black gel food coloring

DIRECTIONS

1. In a mixing bowl, mix the baking soda, citric acid, cornstarch and Epsom salt (dry ingredients). In a separate bowl, mix the castor oil, water, essential oil and the red food coloring (wet ingredients).

2. Slowly pour the wet ingredients into the dry ingredients with one hand while mixing with the other. Do not pour too fast or you will cause the fizzing reaction. You want your mixture to stick together but not be too wet. Once you can grab a handful and it sort of clumps together like wet sand it is ready. If it's too dry, add a few drops of water.

3. Grab your round plastic mold and start packing one side of the mold with the mixture extremely tight; the tighter the better.

4. Add some of the spider sprinkles into the middle of the mold. Complete with the other half of the plastic mold then snap the two sides together. Allow the bath bomb to stay in the mold overnight to dry.

5. Once dry, carefully remove the mold. Take your black food marker and draw a spider web on the top of your bath bomb. Allow the spider web design to dry. You can then place it back into the mold for future use or use it right away.

6. When ready, throw this into the bath and watch the baby spiders hatch before your eyes. The best part is, they will dissolve in the bathtub too!

SOAP SUDS

Rubba, dub, dub—it's time to get into the tub. Don't forget to wash away today's fun-filled day with a little bit of scrub. We'll pop bubbles and level up, all until the sun comes up. Move over loofah because these aquatic cleaning bars are the new sheriff in town. YEEEE-HAW!

Buried Treasure Soap

Yar, there be buried treasure in this sandy soap! "X" marks for the spot for where ye will find the buried gold.

YIELD: 4 soaps

MATERIALS

2 lb (900 g) white glycerin melt-and-pour soap

Condiment bottle

Red gel food coloring

3–4 drops coconut fragrance oil

6-cavity rectangle silicone mold

1 block brown soap color bar

1 tbsp (14 g) dried ground orange peel

99% isopropyl alcohol (in a spray bottle)

4 plastic gold coins

Black gel food coloring

DIRECTIONS

1. Cut the white soap into cubes and place inside of a microwave safe cup. Melt your soap on high in your microwave for 30 seconds then remove and stir. Repeat until all the soap is melted. Be careful not to burn the soap.

2. Pour a tiny amount of the melted white soap into your condiment bottle and add 5 to 6 drops of the red gel food coloring and fragrance oil. Shake to mix.

3. Pour the red melted soap into one of the cavities of the mold in a thin layer. Allow this to harden.

4. Cut off a tiny piece of the brown soap color bar and stir it into the rest of the melted soap from step 1. Add the dried orange peel and stir well.

5. Remove the hardened red soap and cut an X shape out using an X-Acto knife.

6. Now carefully pour the melted soap into your rectangle silicone mold halfway. Give the top of the soap a few sprays of the isopropyl alcohol to help remove any air bubbles and allow to harden for about 30 minutes.

7. Once hardened, spray your gold coin with the isopropyl alcohol. Place the gold coin on top of the first layer of soap.

8. Give the top of the soap a few sprays of the alcohol. Then, pour the remaining amount of soap on top of the gold coin.

9. Before soap hardens, carefully place the red X close to one of the corners of the soap. Do this while the soap is still a little tacky so it sticks and allow to harden for several hours.

10. Once the soap has hardened, gently flip the mold over and push the soap out from the backside. Use the black gel food coloring to add dotted lines to make a trail to the X. Your soap is now ready to use. Wash and dig your way to the hidden treasure inside!

(continued)

Buried Treasure Soap (cont.)

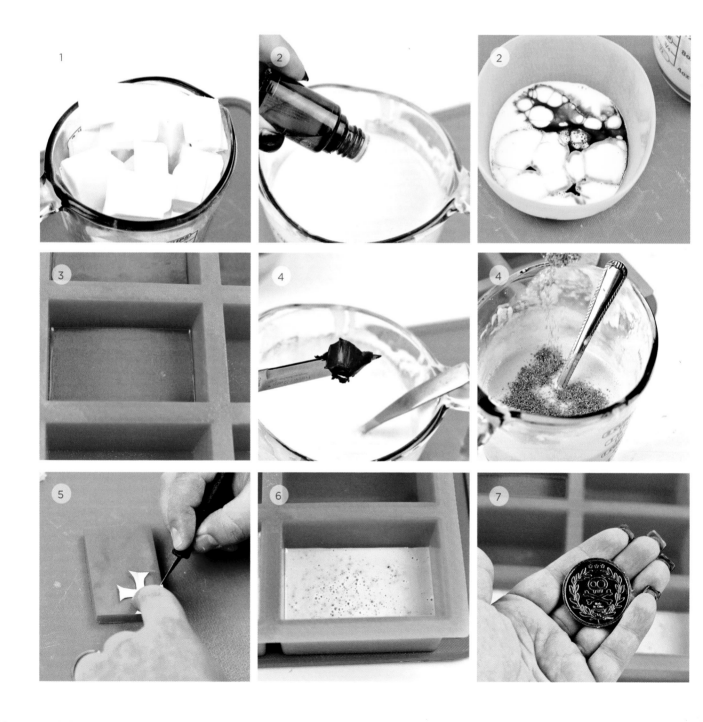

Extraterrestrial Hand Soap

It's a bird, it's a plane, it's an—alien? Not to worry, these little guys come in peace! Well, maybe not to the germs they are about to destroy, but otherwise they are peaceful little guys. This alien hand soap takes washing those little hands (before or after a bath) to an entirely new level. Most likely space but we will try to keep you all grounded.

YIELD: 1 soap dispenser

MATERIALS

Plastic soap dispenser (make sure opening is large enough to stick toy inside)

Mini alien toys (plastic)

Neon blue food coloring (or neon green)

Lime essential oil (optional)

Clear (unscented) liquid hand soap

DIRECTIONS

1. Open the top of the plastic soap dispenser.

2. Add the mini alien toys (I used about 7).

3. Add 1 drop of neon blue food coloring on top of the toys.

4. Add your essential oil (if using). I used about 3 drops.

5. Carefully squeeze the hand soap into your soap dispenser, filling it about ¾ the way full.

6. Give the bottle a good shake to mix the color and essential oil.

7. Enjoy the alien soap you just made (it can be used right away).

(continued)

Extraterrestrial Hand Soap (cont.)

Bat Boomerang Soap

Evildoers beware: Crimes in this tub will not go unpunished. Normal kid by day, shower defender by bath time. I am the one who suds, I am the one who cleans—I AM BATH MAN!

YIELD: About 12 (1-oz [28-g]) bars

MATERIALS

1 lb (450 g) clear glycerin soap

1 cube black soap color bar

2–3 drops lemon essential oil

99% isopropyl alcohol (in a spray bottle)

Bat-shaped cookie cutter (or silicone mold; both can be found at an online retailer, such as Amazon)

DIRECTIONS

1. Cut the clear soap into cubes and place inside of a microwave safe cup. Melt your soap on high in your microwave for 30 seconds then remove and stir. Repeat until all the soap is melted. Be careful not to burn the soap.

2. Cut off small pieces of the black soap color bar and stir it into the melted soap from the previous step. Continue to do this until you achieve a dark black color. Add your essential oil and stir well.

3. Now carefully pour the melted soap onto a flat surface, such as a baking sheet. You only need ½ inch (1 cm).

4. Give the top of the soap a few sprays of the isopropyl alcohol to help remove any air bubbles trapped at the surface. Allow this to harden for several hours.

5. Once the soap has hardened, gently flip the mold over and push the soap out. Use your bat-shaped cookie cutter to cut out the bats.

6. Your soap is now ready to use and ready to help save Batham (the city in the bath).

Brain Shower Jellies

Quick! Board the windows and barricade the doors. The zombies are coming for your BRAINS—jelly brains that is! You can hide in the tub but they will find you if you aren't quick enough to dispose of their favorite snack!

YIELD: 4 shower jellies

MATERIALS

2 packets unflavored gelatin

1 cup (250 ml) boiling distilled water

½ cup (125 ml) clear unscented body wash

1 tsp (6 g) salt

3–4 drops bubblegum fragrance oil

Red food coloring

4-cavity brain silicone mold

DIRECTIONS

1. In a bowl, combine your unflavored gelatin, distilled water and body wash. Stir well. Add the salt and fragrance oil and stir well again.

2. Add several drops of red food coloring until you achieve that dark red color we know all zombies love. Stir this well into the mixture.

3. Carefully pour the mixture into the brain mold, filling each cavity entirely. Place the mold into the fridge for about 2 hours to harden.

4. Once cooled, flip the mold over and gently push out the shower jelly brains.

5. Use them right away in the shower by lathering them up in between your hands. Store any leftovers in the fridge or in a cool, dry place until ready for use.

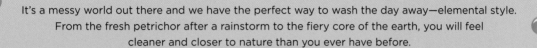

Elemental Soap

It's a messy world out there and we have the perfect way to wash the day away—elemental style. From the fresh petrichor after a rainstorm to the fiery core of the earth, you will feel cleaner and closer to nature than you ever have before.

YIELD: 4 soaps

MATERIALS

1 lb (450 g) clear melt-and-pour soap

Green food coloring

Blue food coloring

Red food coloring

Yellow food coloring

12-cavity rectangle silicone mold

99% isopropyl alcohol (in a spray bottle)

DIRECTIONS

1. Cut the clear soap into cubes and place inside of a microwave safe cup. Melt your soap on high in your microwave for 30 seconds then remove and stir. Repeat until all the soap is melted. Be careful not to burn the soap.

2. Pour a small amount of soap into 4 separate bowls. In the first bowl, add 5 to 10 drops of green food coloring and stir well. Set aside. Repeat this step with the remaining colors.

3. Fill a thin layer of each color into a cavity in the mold. Allow these to harden, which should take about 20 to 30 minutes.

4. In the meantime, fill 4 cavities of your rectangle mold halfway with the clear soap. Once the colored soaps are hard, remove them from the molds and place onto a cutting board.

5. Using an X-Acto knife, cut out the shapes of the elements. For earth, you'll cut out a small leaf. For the water, you'll cut out a small rain drop. For the red, you'll cut out a small flame and for the yellow, you'll cut out a small lightning bolt.

6. Once the elements are cut out, spray them with isopropyl alcohol and place them into the middle of the half-filled rectangle molds. Pour the remaining amount of the clear melted soap on top (make sure this isn't too hot or it will melt the elemental part of the soap).

7. Allow this all to harden before removing from the mold (overnight is best). Once hard, remove from the mold and place them onto a cutting board. Grab a knife and start to cut off pieces in the corners so you form a crystal-like shape. You can even cut off small parts in the middle. Have fun with this and make each one a different shape and size. You will have different elemental soaps!

(continued)

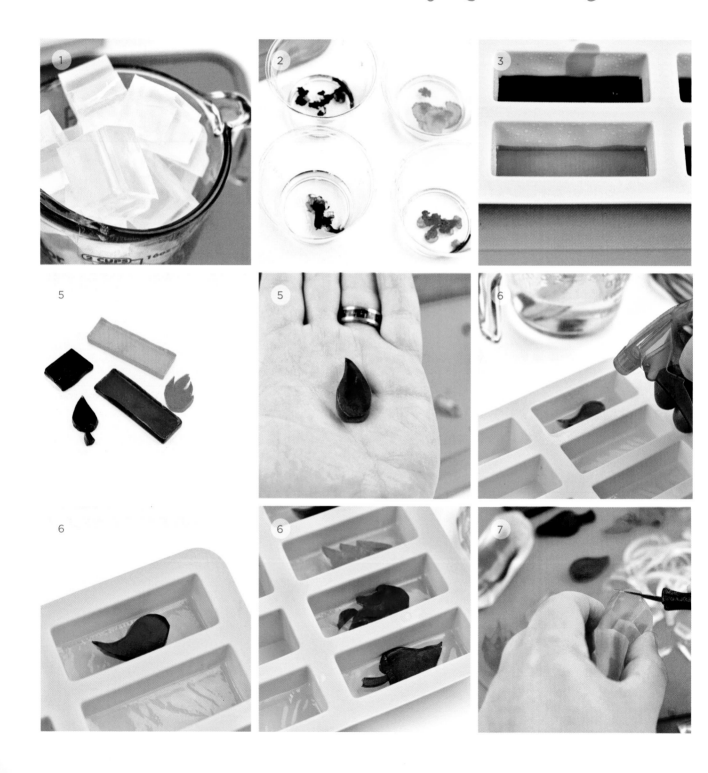

Chocolate Frog Soap

You will be as giddy as a wizard with this chocolate frog soap. While this one doesn't come with a wizard card, it sure can jump. Be careful that chocolate frog doesn't slip away out of the tub because you'll be left with a splashy mess and no way to get clean!

YIELD: 8 soaps

MATERIALS

1 lb (450 g) white glycerin melt-and-pour soap

1 block brown soap color bar

2-3 drops chocolate fragrance oil

Chocolate frog plastic candy molds (can be found at an online retailer, such as Amazon)

99% isopropyl alcohol (in a spray bottle)

Gold sparkle mica

DIRECTIONS

1. Cut the white soap into cubes and place inside of a microwave safe cup. Melt your soap on high in your microwave for 30 seconds then remove and stir. Repeat until all the soap is melted. Be careful not to burn the soap.

2. Cut a small piece of the brown soap color bar off and place it into the melted soap.

3. Stir well. If the brown isn't dark enough, add a bit more until you get that milk chocolate color. Add your chocolate fragrance oil and stir well. You only need a few drops since this scent is quite strong.

4. Now carefully pour the melted soap into your chocolate frog molds.

5. Spray the tops of the frogs with the isopropyl alcohol to remove any air bubbles on the surface. Allow these to harden overnight or you can speed up the process by placing them into the fridge for a few hours.

6. Once hardened, remove them by gently pressing on the backside of the mold. Now take a paintbrush and dip it into the gold sparkle mica. Gently paint on the gold mica to give the chocolate frogs a shiny effect.

7. When ready, you can use this soap in the shower and come out smelling like chocolate!

(continued)

Chocolate
Frog Soap (cont.)

Constellation Soap

Astronomers will be amazed at how quickly you'll find your zodiac sign in the starry night. One use of this soap and you will shine bright like the North Star and be closer to the Big Dipper than anyone ever has before. A truly giant step for mankind.

YIELD: 4 soaps

MATERIALS

1 lb (450 g) white glycerin melt-and-pour soap

2–3 drops blue food coloring

1–2 drops purple food coloring

2–3 drops grape fragrance oil

1 tsp (5 g) iridescent super sparkle glitter (skin-safe)

8-cavity square silicone mold

White star sprinkles

White gel food coloring

DIRECTIONS

1. Cut the white soap into cubes and place inside of a microwave safe cup. Melt your soap on high in your microwave for 30 seconds then remove and stir. Repeat until all the soap is melted. Be careful not to burn the soap.

2. Next add the blue and purple food coloring to the melted soap and give it a nice twirl. You should end up with a dark blueish purple color (almost black). Add your grape fragrance oil and your glitter and stir well.

3. Now carefully pour the melted soap into 4 cavities of the mold, and allow your soap time to cool overnight. Once hardened, remove them by gently pressing on the backside of the mold.

4. Once the soaps are removed, add the star sprinkles by gently wetting the back and then placing them onto the top of the soap. Connect the sprinkles with the white gel food coloring to make constellations.

5. You can use these immediately or wrap in plastic wrap until ready to use.

Critical Hit Soap

I bet when you woke up this morning you didn't think your fate would be in the hands of a die. With a bit of luck and the right fling of the wrist, you might just find the answer you've been seeking. Roll the wrong number and you might just be doomed.

YIELD: 1 soap

MATERIALS

½ lb (225 g) white glycerin melt-and-pour soap

2–3 drops lemon essential oil

D20 dice silicone mold

99% isopropyl alcohol (in a spray bottle)

DIRECTIONS

1. Lay your cutting board onto a flat surface. Take your knife or soap cutter and cut the white soap into cubes and place inside of your microwave safe cup. Melt your soap on high in your microwave for 30 seconds then remove and stir. Repeat until all the soap is melted. Be careful not to burn the soap.

2. Add your lemon essential oil and stir well.

3. Grab your mold and remove the top (you won't need this part for the soap).

4. Carefully pour the melted white soap into the mold, filling it entirely. Since the top of the mold will be flat, this will become the bottom of your soap once removed. Spray the top with isopropyl alcohol to remove any air bubbles on the surface.

5. Allow the soap to harden for 24 hours before removing. To remove, gently push from the backside of the silicone mold and it will pop right out.

6. You can repeat this process and make several different dice and even add food coloring or soap colorant to make them different colors!

7. When ready, get to using this soap and your fate will be delivered.

Dino Dig Soap

Explore the world of the dinosaurs. Clean, wash and excavate your way to your favorite dinosaur skeleton. Once you've dug your way into your bar of soap, you will find what has been buried for millions of years. This is the perfect alterative to all the mess endured at a real excavation site but with all the same fun.

YIELD: About 4 soaps (depending on the size of mold you use)

MATERIALS

1 lb (450 g) white glycerin soap base

Oakmoss fragrance oil (or skin-safe oil of your choosing)

1 block brown soap color bar

⅛ cup (28 g) coffee grounds, optional

Rectangle plastic soap mold

99% isopropyl alcohol (in a spray bottle)

Fossil figure toys

DIRECTIONS

1. Start by cutting your white soap base into small chunks. Then place into a microwave safe measuring cup or bowl. Microwave the soap for 30 seconds, remove and stir. Complete this process until all soap is melted. Once this soap is melted, add the oakmoss or any fragrance oil you wish to use. Stir well.

2. Next, add your colorant. Start with half of the block of colorant and increase to reach your desired shade (go for a natural dirt color). Stir well until all color is melted and well blended.

3. Add your coffee grounds to the soap and stir well. Allow the soap to cool a bit and then stir again so the coffee grounds will be evenly suspended throughout. This step is optional but gives more of an appearance of dirt.

4. Pour about a half inch (13.5 mm) of soap into each cavity of your soap mold. Then spray the top with isopropyl alcohol.

5. Allow the soap to harden then proceed to the next steps.

6. Spray the fossil toys with isopropyl alcohol. This step is necessary to allow the soap to stick to the toy.

7. Pour the remaining melted soap on top of the fossil toy until it's covered entirely. The idea is to have the toy buried inside the dirt.

8. Allow this to harden for several hours (overnight is ideal).

9. Once the soap has completely hardened, remove it from the mold by gently pressing the backside of the mold until the soap releases.

10. Use the soap immediately or store in an airtight container or wrap in plastic wrap until ready for use.

(continued)

Dino Dig Soap (cont.)

Fairy Wing Soap Petals

Straight from the forest these wings come, dazzled and delighted to help you fly! Fairies know all the secrets of the woodlands, which includes the perfect recipe for washing little hands. Just a dash of fairy dust and a bit of soap will make you as clean and magical as a fairy in no time.

YIELD: 6 soap petals

MATERIALS

Small fairy or butterfly wings (the kind with wire and fabric)

½ lb (227 g) clear melt-and-pour soap

2–3 drops lavender essential oil

DIRECTIONS

1. Cut the fairy or butterfly wings in half vertically so you have the wings separated.

2. Cut the clear soap into cubes and place inside of a microwave safe cup. Melt your soap on high in your microwave for 30 seconds then remove and stir. Repeat until all the soap is melted. Be careful not to burn the soap.

3. Add your lavender essential oil and stir well.

4. Lay a piece of wax paper flat onto your counter. Using a spoon, dip the fairy wings into the melted soap so it covers the wing entirely. You still should be able to see the wing through the soap.

5. Carefully take the dipped fairy wing from the bowl and lay it onto the wax paper (wax side up) to dry.

6. Allow these to harden for about an hour before use. If you have excess soap around the sides you can gently break it off or cut using a butter knife.

7. When ready to use, just rub the fairy wing between your hands and you will be clean just like magic.

(continued)

Fairy Wing
Soap Petals (cont.)

Galaxy Shower Jelly

Travel to the darkest depths of the galaxy like no human has ever done before. This shower jelly will get you sparkly clean, but beware of those black holes, for this will then be gone faster than the speed of light.

YIELD: 6 shower jellies

MATERIALS

2 packets unflavored gelatin

1 cup (250 ml) boiling distilled water

½ cup (125 ml) clear unscented body wash

1 tsp (6 g) salt

3–4 drops lemon essential oil

2 tbsp (28 g) iridescent super sparkle glitter (skin-safe)

Purple food coloring

Blue food coloring

Pink food coloring

Round 6-cavity silicone muffin pan mold

DIRECTIONS

1. In a bowl, combine the unflavored gelatin, distilled water and body wash. Stir well. Add the salt, essential oil and the glitter and stir well again. Separate the mixture into 3 small bowls.

2. In the first bowl, add 2 to 3 drops of purple food coloring and stir well. Repeat this step with the remaining colors and bowls.

3. Take the first bowl of colored mixture and pour a tiny bit into one of the mold cavities. Repeat with each cavity.

4. Next, pour the second color into each cavity, filling it only a little.

5. Finally, pour the third and last color into each cavity, filling it entirely. The idea is to have this swirled effect of colors (like the galaxy).

6. Place the mold into the fridge for about 2 hours to harden. Once cooled, flip the mold over and gently push out the shower jellies.

7. Use them right away in the shower by lathering them up in between your hands. Store any leftovers in the fridge or in a cool, dry place until ready for use.

Hungry Man Soap

Germs and ghosts don't stand a chance! You will bite and chomp your way through those tiny curves and creases with this soap. The big yellow man is hungry and will leave no crumbs behind.

YIELD: 3 soaps

MATERIALS

1 lb (450 g) white glycerin soap base

1 block yellow soap color bar

Banana fragrance oil

4-cavity round silicone mold

White gel food coloring

3 small candy eyes (1 per soap)

DIRECTIONS

1. Cut the white soap into cubes and place inside a microwave safe cup. Melt your soap on high in your microwave for 30 seconds then remove and stir. Repeat until all the soap is melted. Be careful not to burn the soap.

2. Add about half of your yellow soap color bar to the melted soap and stir until it is well melted. You want it to be a bright yellow so if you need to darken it, add more of the colorant. Add your fragrance oil and stir well.

3. Pour the melted soap into 3 cavities of your round silicone mold and allow to harden overnight. When ready, gently press from the backside of the mold to remove the soap and place onto a cutting board.

4. Take a sharp knife and cut out a triangle (this will now become hungry man's smiling mouth).

5. Take your white gel food coloring and apply a small dot of it on top of the soap. Add the candy on top for the eye.

6. Allow the food dye to dry and then your soap is ready for use. Watch out because he's hungry and ready to eat!

(continued)

Hungry Man Soap (cont.)

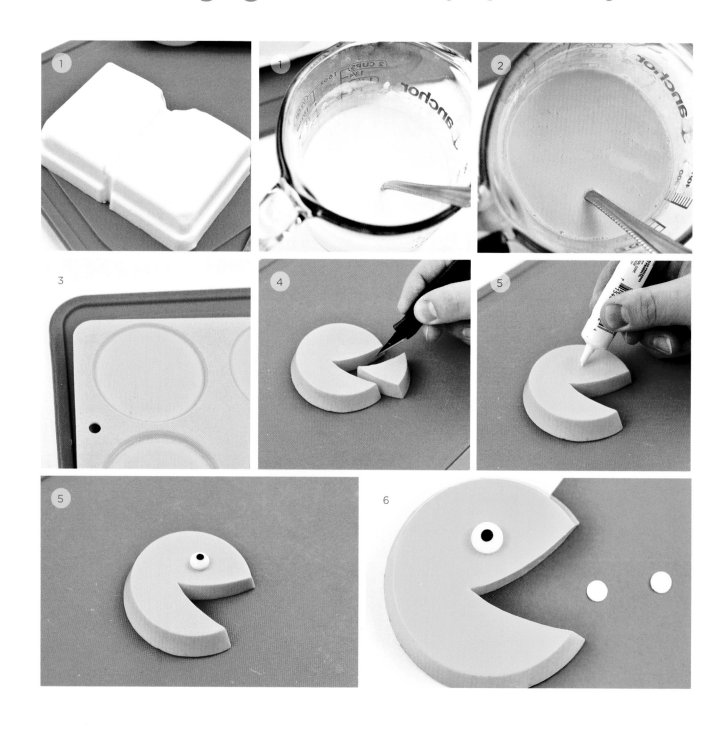

Mystery Box Soap

Everything is more fun when it is a mystery because anything can be inside. Could be a flower, could be a star, could even be a shiny gold coin. Hang onto those surprises tight so they don't go down the drain.

YIELD: 4 soaps

MATERIALS

2 lb (900 g) white glycerin melt-and-pour soap

Square cake pan silicone mold

1 block yellow soap color bar

3–4 drops lemon essential oil

6-cavity square silicone mold

99% isopropyl alcohol (in a spray bottle)

4 plastic gold coin toys (1 per soap)

Straw

DIRECTIONS

1. Cut the white soap into cubes and place inside of your microwave safe cup. Melt your soap on high in your microwave for 30 seconds then remove and stir. Repeat until all the soap is melted. Be careful not to burn the soap.

2. Pour a very small layer (about ½ inch [13.5 mm]) into the bottom of the square silicone cake pan and allow to harden for about 30 minutes. Once the soap has hardened, remove from the mold and lay flat onto a cutting board.

3. Take a knife and cut question mark shapes out of the white soap then place one mirror image on the bottom of each of the square cavities (you'll need 4). Next, add about half of your yellow soap color bar to the remaining amount of the melted soap and stir until it is melted. You want it to be a bright yellow. If you need to reheat the soap you can. Add your essential oil and stir well.

4. Pour half of the melted soap into your square silicone molds and allow to harden for about 30 minutes. Make sure this isn't too hot or it will melt the white question mark at the bottom.

5. Next, spray the layer of yellow soap with the isopropyl alcohol and then spray the gold coin and lay on top of the first layer of soap. Pour the remaining melted yellow soap on top to fill each cavity.

6. Allow your soap to harden overnight then carefully remove from the mold. The white question mark will be at the top.

7. Take a straw and carefully carve out 4 small corners in top of the soap to give it that boxed look. When ready to bathe, bust that baby out and you will have all sorts of fun!

(continued)

Mystery
Box Soap (cont.)

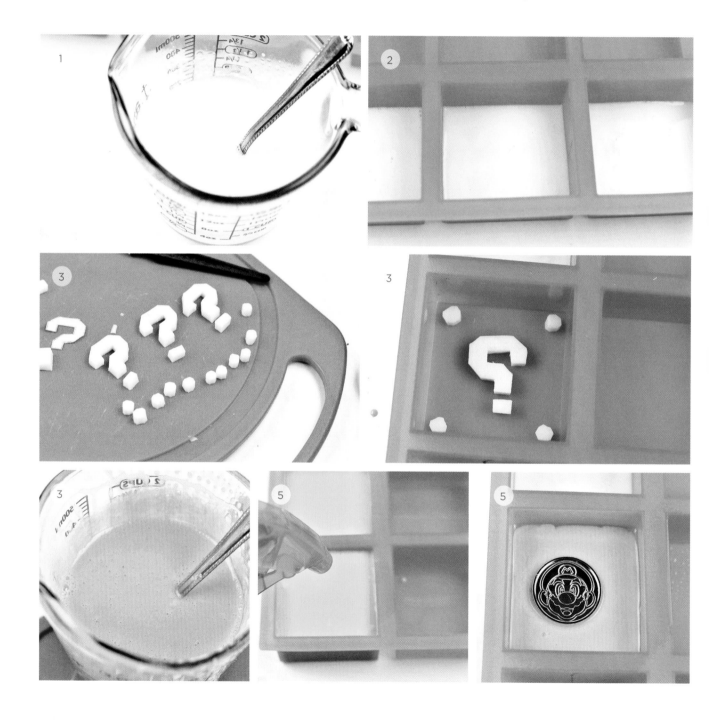

Sea Hamburger Soap

Enjoy this anywhere—on a boat, under the sea, even in the bath? That's right! World famous meals now come in large, xtra large and SOAP! The best part is, you don't have to go under the sea to get one (something that greedy crab won't appreciate). You can make it in your very own home, but be careful to keep the recipe away from tiny green planktons.

YIELD: 4 soaps

MATERIALS

2 lb (900 g) clear glycerin melt-and-pour soap

3–4 drops lemon essential oil

Red food coloring

6-cavity rectangle silicone mold

Mini fast-food erasers

99% isopropyl alcohol (in a spray bottle)

DIRECTIONS

1. Cut the clear soap into cubes and place inside of a microwave safe cup. Melt your soap on high in your microwave for 30 seconds then remove. Repeat until all the soap is melted. Be careful not to burn the soap.

2. Pour about ¼ of the clear soap into a bowl and add several drops of your essential oil and red food coloring. Stir well. You want a good solid red color (think Santa red).

3. Pour a very thin layer of this red colored soap into the bottom of the mold. This will become the food tray for your soap.

4. Before the red soap hardens entirely, place several of the fast-food erasers vertically on top of the red soap. Spray with isopropyl alcohol until it is covered well. This helps the layers adhere to each other.

5. Now it's time to finish off the soap! Pour the remaining clear soap on top of the erasers, filling the mold entirely.

6. Allow the soap to harden overnight. When hard, remove from the mold by gently pressing on the backside until the soap is released.

7. You can use it right away. It will be so fun to play with you might just want to eat it (but make sure you don't!).

Mermaid Shell Shower Jellies

Is it another dinglehopper? No, it's a mermaid shower jelly straight from under the sea. Down where it's wetter, the shells are shinier and only in the shower, there will be a mermaid from under the sea!

YIELD: 4 shower jellies

MATERIALS

2 packets unflavored gelatin

1 cup (250 ml) boiling distilled water

½ cup (125 ml) clear unscented body wash

1 tsp (6 g) salt

3–4 drops ocean rain fragrance oil

6–8 drops purple food coloring

2 tbsp (28 g) iridescent super sparkle glitter (skin-safe)

Half shell plastic soap mold

DIRECTIONS

1. In a bowl, combine your unflavored gelatin, distilled water and body wash. Stir well. Add the salt, fragrance oil, food coloring and glitter and stir well again.

2. Pour the mixture into each shell mold, filling them entirely. Place the mold into the fridge for about 2 hours to harden.

3. Once cooled, flip the mold over and gently push out the shower jellies.

4. Use these thingamabobbers right away in the shower by lathering them up in between your hands.

5. Store any leftovers in the fridge or in a cool, dry place until ready for use.

Phoenix Feather Soap

Burst from the flames and arise from the ashes like a newborn chick. This phoenix feather soap will leave you feeling immune to the gaze of a basilisk. The red, orange and yellow crimson colors of this soap will bestow the essence of the loyalty of a phoenix.

YIELD: 6 soaps

MATERIALS

1 lb (450 g) clear glycerin soap base

2-3 drops birds of paradise fragrance oil (or other skin-safe essential oil or fragrance oil)

2 drops of yellow food coloring

Red and orange colored feathers

Rectangular silicone 9-cavity soap mold

99% isopropyl alcohol antiseptic solution in a spray bottle

DIRECTIONS

1. Cut your melt and pour soap into cubes and place into a microwave safe bowl. Heat for 30 seconds in the microwave, stir and repeat until melted. Do not allow the soap to burn.

2. Add your fragrance. You will only need a few drops. Stir well.

3. Add the yellow food coloring and give it a quick swirl but don't entirely mix the color into the soap. Place the red and orange feathers into the bottom of 6 cavities of your mold. You can cut your feathers to fit into the mold if needed.

4. Carefully pour the melted soap over the top of the feathers, filling each cavity entirely. Spray the surface of the soaps with the isopropyl alcohol to remove any air bubbles.

5. Leave in the mold to harden overnight.

6. Once the soap has hardened, gently push from the backside of the mold to release. You can then use the soap immediately or wrap in plastic wrap for future use.

(continued)

Pheonix Feather
Soap (cont.)

Smart Mouth Anti-Hero Soap

He's a good guy, he's a bad guy, nobody really knows. One thing is for certain, he has a witty personality and a solid appetite for chimichangas. Kicking butt in a tight red and black suit all day really breaks a sweat. Only a soap with as much sass as he has can really clean.

YIELD: 4 soaps

MATERIALS

2 lb (900 g) clear glycerin melt-and-pour soap

3–4 drops lemon essential oil

5–6 drops red food coloring

½ block black soap colorant

8-cavity round silicone mold

Oval cookie cutter

Straw

3 oz (85 g) white glycerin melt-and-pour soap

Plastic pipette

DIRECTIONS

1. Cut the clear soap into cubes and place inside a microwave safe cup. Melt your soap on high in your microwave for 30 seconds then remove and stir. Repeat until all the soap is melted. Be careful not to burn the soap. Add your essential oil and stir well.

2. Pour half of the melted soap into another bowl. In the first bowl, add your red food coloring and stir well. In the second bowl, add your black soap colorant and set aside.

3. Pour the black colored mixture into 4 of the round molds. You only want a thin layer for the details of the eyes. Allow this to harden.

4. Once the black soap has hardened, remove from the mold and cut out oval pieces using the cookie cutter.

5. Next, use a straw to cut out small round sections from the oval pieces. These will become the inside of the eyes.

6. Melt the white melt and pour soap and use the plastic pipette to carefully fill the inside of the eyes with the white melted soap. It may be easier to place the black pieces into the round silicone mold before doing this. Allow to harden.

7. Once the white soap has hardened, and your eyes are in place inside the round silicone mold, reheat the red soap and carefully pour over the details of the face.

8. Allow this to harden overnight then remove from the molds. You should have a really cool face that looks like just the anti-hero!

(continued)

Princess Shampoo

Well, glitter me princess! This shampoo will have Prince Charming asking about your lovely locks. Besides, who doesn't want the most beautiful hair in the land for that princess crown to sit upon? Just don't lose your slipper in the process of getting clean!

YIELD: 1 shampoo bottle

MATERIALS

1½ cups (355 ml) clear unscented shampoo (or 2-in-1 body wash)

1 tsp (5 g) iridescent super sparkle glitter (skin safe)

1 drop neon pink food coloring

2 drops bubblegum fragrance oil

Plastic shampoo bottle

Mini plastic princess heels

DIRECTIONS

1. In a bowl, combine the shampoo, glitter, food coloring and fragrance oil. Mix well.

2. Pour half of the shampoo mixture into your plastic shampoo bottle. Add about 10 of the princess heels into the shampoo bottle.

3. Fill the bottle with the remaining shampoo solution and secure the lid on top.

4. Let your adorable little princess bathe and wash her lovely locks. She'll surely come out smelling like a bubblegum-scented rose.

Time to Wash Hand Soap

I'm late, I'm late, for a very important bath! Don't slip down that slippery rabbit hole. Beware of the hatter and hare, for if you don't watch the time you could be swept away into the lair of the deadly queen.

YIELD: 1 hand soap

MATERIALS

Plastic soap dispenser (make sure opening is large enough to put the beads inside)

Clear (unscented) liquid hand soap (you need enough to fill the bottle you chose)

2–3 drops lavender essential oil, optional

Mini clock beads (can be found at an online retailer, such as Amazon)

DIRECTIONS

1. Open the top of the plastic soap dispenser. Pour in the liquid hand soap and fill the bottle about halfway full before adding in the essential oil.

2. Add the clock beads. Fill the bottle with the remaining amount of hand soap.

3. Give the bottle a good shake to mix the beads around.

4. You can then be on time to your hand-washing party.

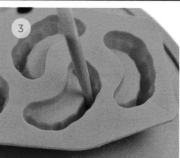

Vampire Fang Soap

These fangs look so real they might as well take a bite of your skin. Don't worry though, this is all just an illusion. They really just want to help you get so clean you look invisible when you stand in front of a mirror!

YIELD: 4 soaps

MATERIALS

1 lb (450 g) white glycerin soap base

2–3 drops strawberry fragrance oil

5–10 drops red food coloring

Plastic pipette

Vampire fang silicone mold (can be found at an online retailer, such as Amazon)

DIRECTIONS

1. Cut the white soap into cubes and place inside a microwave safe cup. Melt your soap on high in your microwave for 30 seconds then remove and stir. Repeat until all the soap is melted. Be careful not to burn the soap. Add your fragrance oil and stir well.

2. Pour about ¼ of the soap into another bowl and add the red food coloring. Stir well.

3. Take your plastic pipette and place a small amount of the red colored soap into the very bottom of the fang part of the mold. You want only the tips to be colored red, like a vampire just took a bite out of something.

4. Fill the mold with the remaining white melted soap.

5. Allow to harden overnight then remove from the mold by gently pressing on the backside of the mold until the soap releases.

6. Share with all your vampire friends and make your nightly bath one to remember!

Weakening Space Crystal Soap

If you are a superhero who thought you could hide behind a pair of glasses and a suit, think again! This green glowing crystal isn't safe for those from outer space and even the slightest touch will weaken any superhero powers you possess. For the rest of us, it's a tool we can use to get clean and make sure we are always feeling our best.

YIELD: 3 soaps

MATERIALS

2 lb (900 g) clear glycerin melt-and-pour soap

3–4 drops lime essential oil

5–6 drops neon green food coloring

1–2 drops yellow food coloring

6-cavity rectangle silicone mold

DIRECTIONS

1. Cut the clear soap into cubes and place inside a microwave safe cup. Melt your soap on high in your microwave for 30 seconds then remove and stir. Repeat until all the soap is melted. Be careful not to burn the soap. Add your essential oil and food coloring and stir well.

2. Pour the melted soap into the rectangle molds, filling them entirely. Allow these to harden overnight before removing.

3. Once removed, place them onto a cutting board and grab your knife. Start to cut off pieces in the corners so you form a crystal-like shape. You can even cut off small parts in the middle. Have fun with this and make each one a different shape and size.

4. When ready, take a shower and watch that green glowing soap weaken those around you!

Werewolf Hunter Soap

It can be dangerous during a full moon and when you hear that howling, be glad that you have your silver bullets by your side even in the shower. These babies will keep the werewolves at bay and wash away the smell of fear that lingers into the night.

YIELD: About 10 (1-oz [28-g]) bars (depending on size of mold used)

MATERIALS

1 lb (450 g) white glycerin soap base

2–3 drops lemon essential oil

1 black soap colorant bar

1 tbsp (14 g) pearly white mica

3D bullet mold (can be found at an online retailer, such as Amazon)

99% isopropyl alcohol (in a spray bottle)

DIRECTIONS

1. Cut your melt-and-pour soap into cubes and place into a microwave safe bowl. Heat for 30 seconds in the microwave, stir and repeat until melted. Do not allow the soap to burn. Add your essential oil. You will only need a few drops. Stir well.

2. Add a small piece of the black soap colorant bar to the melted white soap and stir well. You should end up with a nice grey color. Add your pearly white mica and stir well.

3. Carefully pour the melted soap into the bullet mold. Spray the surface of the soaps with the isopropyl alcohol to remove any air bubbles.

4. Leave in the mold to harden overnight. Once the soap has hardened, gently push from the backside of the mold to release.

5. You can then use the soap immediately or wrap in plastic wrap for future use when there is a full moon in sight!

SCRUBBA LUBBA DUB DUB

What makes everything better? Sugar! Now what makes everything sweet? More sugar! So when you combine sugar and sugar you get a perfectly crafted sugar scrub so moisturizing and exfoliating you could scrub yourself right into a time warp. If that happens, you'll want to stay away from your past and future selves.

1

2

2

2

3

8-Bit Dynamite Foaming Sugar Scrub

BOOM! goes the dynamite. Clearing out all the skeletons, creepers and spiders before your nightly bath has never been easier. Just take one of these from your inventory, plop it into your bath and watch the explosive fun. Disclaimer: No little fingers and toes are harmed in the process.

YIELD: 1 sugar scrub

MATERIALS

1 tbsp (15 ml) grapeseed oil

1 tbsp (14 g) red mica

1 cup (225 g) foaming bath whip

1 cup (225 g) granulated sugar

3-4 drops redwood and saffron fragrance oil

Clear plastic favor or cupcake box (3 x 3 x 3-inch [7 x 7 x 7-cm] size will work)

Small piece of black string or pipe cleaner

White piece of paper

Black permanent marker

Tape

DIRECTIONS

1. In a small bowl, combine the grapeseed oil and red mica. Stir well then set aside.

2. In a larger bowl, combine the foaming bath whip and granulated sugar. It is easier if you use a hand mixer to combine these. Add the red mica colored oil and the fragrance oil and mix well. You should now have a nice brick red color.

3. Scoop the mixture into your plastic favor box, filling it entirely. Place a small piece of black string on the top to make it look like the wick to the dynamite. Close up the package and then grab your white piece of paper. Cut a thin piece off the paper and write "TNT" on it using the black marker.

4. Tape this to the front and be ready to watch your foam sugar scrub in the bath. Just toss in a few spoonfuls and the dynamite will come to life!

Grinning Cat Sugar Scrub

Mischievous grins this sugar scrub will have. We're all mad with the grinning cat and his cunning ways. Is it good or bad? This sugar scrub will leave you wondering just how soft your skin can be and don't be alarmed if you disappear suddenly.

YIELD: 1 sugar scrub

MATERIALS

2 cups (450 g) granulated sugar

1 cup (250 ml) grapeseed oil

3 drops bubblegum fragrance oil

Pink food dye gel

Purple food dye gel

Clear jar with a lid

Pink & purple foam sheets

2 googly eyes

DIRECTIONS

1. Combine the sugar, grapeseed oil and fragrance oil in a bowl and stir well. Divide the mixture equally into 2 separate bowls.

2. In the first bowl, add 5 to 10 drops of the pink food dye gel and stir well. You want to achieve a bright pink color.

3. Next, add 5 to 10 drops of the purple food dye gel to the other bowl.

4. Layer the mixtures by alternating colors until the entire jar is filled with the sugar scrub. You want it to be striped just like the famous grinning cat.

5. You can leave it as is or attach a grinning face made from the foam sheets (ears, mouth and tail) and googly eyes to the outside of the jar.

6. When ready, add a spoonful of the scrub to the bath and watch the magic happen right before your eyes.

(continued)

Ninja Sugar Scrub

(By Holly Homer from Kids Activities Blog at http://kidsactivitiesblog.com)

If you thought that ninjas couldn't take baths like the rest of us, let me karate kick an idea to your mind. With your cat-like reflexes and a dash of this scrub, you will be in and out of the bath so fast, nobody with ever have known you were there.

YIELD: 1 sugar scrub

MATERIALS

2 cups (450 g) granulated sugar

1 cup (250 ml) grapeseed oil

3 drops lemon essential oil

Red gel food dye

Black gel food dye

2 googly eyes

Hot glue gun and glue

Clear jar with lid

Mini ninja sword, for decoration, optional

DIRECTIONS

1. Combine the sugar, grapeseed oil and essential oil in a bowl and stir well.

2. Take about ¼ of the sugar scrub mixture and place into another bowl. Place 3 to 5 drops of red gel food dye into the mixture, and stir well.

3. Add 2 to 3 drops of the black gel food dye to the remainder of the sugar scrub mixture and stir until well combined.

4. Layer two-thirds of the black sugar scrub into your jar. Next, add the red layer of the sugar scrub. Add the final layer of the black sugar scrub so that your jar is filled entirely.

5. Hot glue the googly eyes to the outside of the jar along where the red layer of sugar scrub is. You now have an awesome stealth-like ninja sugar scrub! Just add a spoonful to your next bath and you'll know what it's like to soak like a ninja!

 TIP: Want to mix it up a little? Next time try using green gel food dye for the body and then red, orange, purple or blue for the area of the eyes to show off your favorite ninja.

(continued)

Ninja Sugar Scub (cont.)

Stackable Puzzle Piece Sugar Scrub Bars

Stack and match by color for fun. Can you find the missing piece to the puzzle? Stack them all before time runs out to complete the round. Beware of a stack too high or it will fall into the tub. By the end, you'll be puzzled at how soft your skin will be.

YIELD: About 6 sugar scrub bars (depending on the size of the mold)

MATERIALS

1 lb (450 g) clear glycerin melt-and-pour soap

3 tbsp (40 g) coconut oil

1 cup (225 g) granulated sugar

4–5 drops strawberry fragrance oil

Red food coloring

Yellow food coloring

Orange food coloring

Blue food coloring

Neon purple food coloring

Green food coloring

Stacking blocks silicone mold

DIRECTIONS

1. Cut your melt and pour soap into cubes and place into a microwave safe bowl with the coconut oil. Heat for 30 seconds in the microwave, stir and repeat until melted. Do not allow the soap to burn. Stir in your sugar and fragrance oil until well combined.

2. Separate the melted mixture into 5 bowls (equal portions). Start coloring the first bowl with the red food coloring. You will need about 10 drops to achieve a dark red color.

3. Repeat the step above with the remaining colors. The more you use, the darker the color will be, but be careful not to use too much.

4. Start pouring the colored mixtures into a cavity of the stacking blocks silicone mold. Color one red, one green, one yellow, etc. Allow these to harden overnight.

5. In the morning, remove by gently pressing from the backside of the mold. When ready, just use these in the shower. They work just like soap but gently exfoliate your skin leaving it silky smooth.

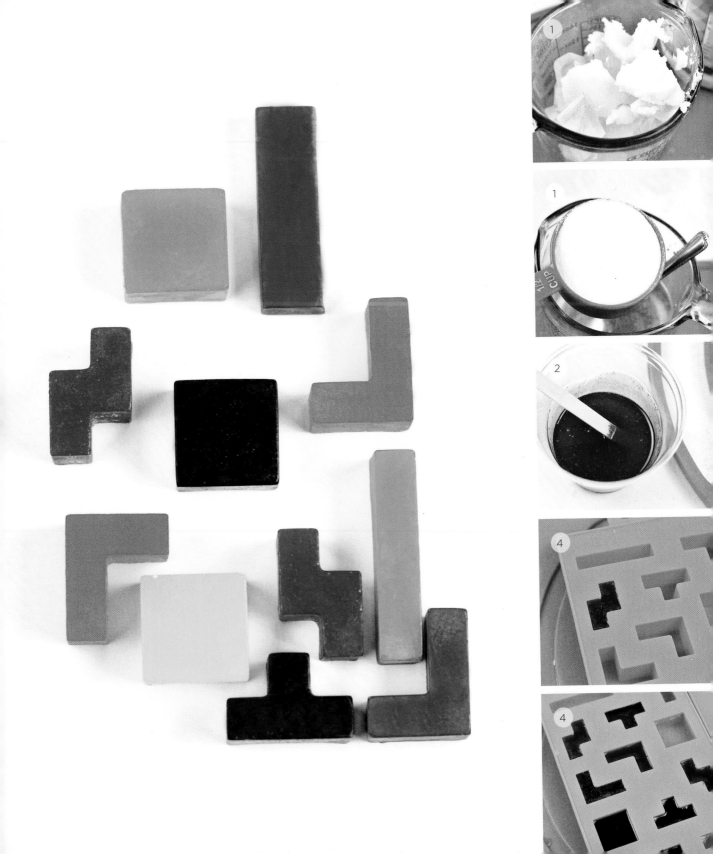

Unicorn Poop Sugar Scrub

(By Jamie Harrington from Totally The Bomb blog at http://totallythebomb.com)

Unicorns are real and there is colorful, glittery poop to prove it. Despite what you might think, it smells like wads of freshly chewed bubblegum that have the magical ability to clean your body. Yeah, it's that awesome!

YIELD: 1 sugar scrub

MATERIALS

2 cups (383 g) granulated sugar

1 cup (218 g) coconut oil

4–5 drops bubblegum fragrance oil

10 drops neon pink gel food dye

10 drops purple gel food dye

10 drops orange gel food dye

Clear jar with lid

Pastel confetti sprinkle stars

DIRECTIONS

1. In a bowl, combine the sugar, coconut oil and fragrance oil. Stir well. Split the sugar mixture equally into 4 bowls.

2. In the first bowl, add 10 drops of the neon pink food dye gel and stir well. Repeat this step with the remaining bowls and colors.

3. Now grab your jar and start to layer the pink sugar scrub until you have about a ½-inch (13-mm) layer.

4. Next add a small layer of the candy sprinkles (add these toward the outer edge so they can be seen through the jar). Repeat the layering with the remaining colors until the jar is full.

5. You can sprinkle one final layer of sprinkles on top and then add the lid.

6. Your unicorn poop sugar scrub is now ready for use and ready to turn your bath into a rainbow of colors!

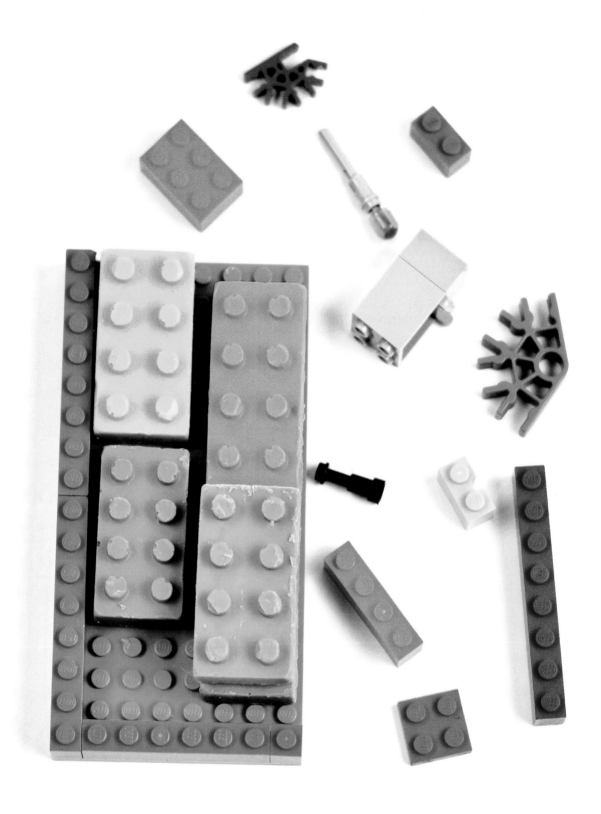

CREATIVE COLORING

Swirly, twirly paint drops—oh what can they be? Draw it out and you will see just how happy one parent can be! Creative fun is for everyone, especially with crayons and bath paints such as these. A blank canvas awaits your epic masterpiece, much like soil waits for a magic bean.

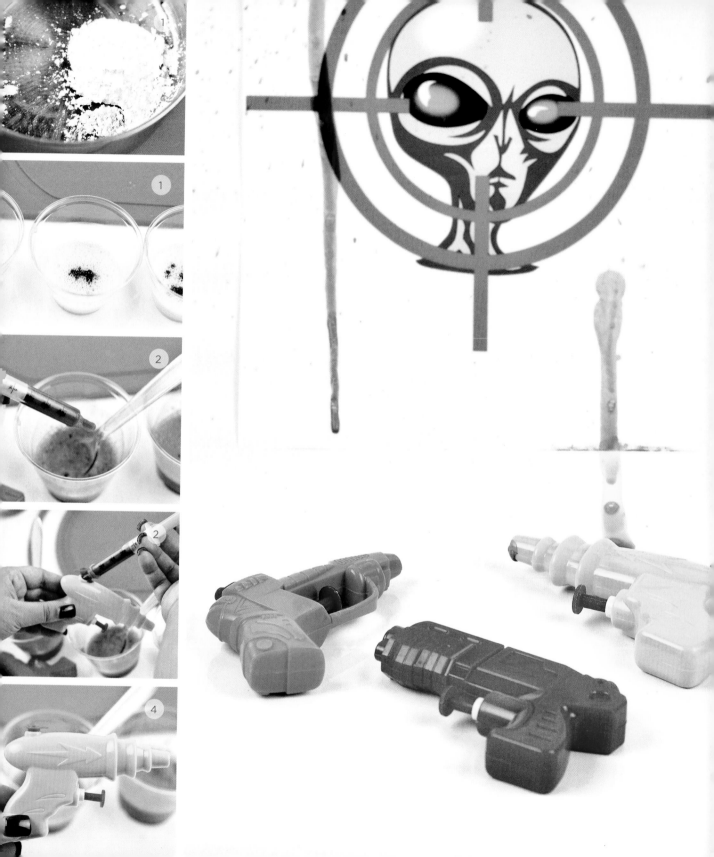

Alien Blaster Paints

While alien abductions in the bathtub are rare, you don't want to be empty-handed if they do show up. Keep these alien basters at your side and when the time comes, strike them with loads of colorful paints. Yes, we've totally heard that aliens dislike bright and beautiful colors, so the more color the better!

YIELD: 1 paint

MATERIALS

¼ cup (60 ml) baby shampoo

1 tbsp (14 g) cornstarch

1 tsp (5 ml) water

Red food coloring

Mini water squirt guns (can find at the dollar store)

Small funnel or syringe

Blue food coloring

Yellow food coloring

Green food coloring

DIRECTIONS

1. In a plastic cup, mix the baby shampoo, cornstarch and water. Add 3 to 4 drops of red food coloring and mix well.

2. Grab a squirt gun and fill it with the shampoo mixture. You can use a funnel or syringe depending on how large the opening to the squirt gun is.

3. Repeat the steps above with the remaining food colors. You can mix red and yellow food coloring to make orange and red and blue to make purple.

4. Once all of your squirt guns are filled, blast all those alien invaders away by squirting the bath paints on the walls of your tub and shower.

5. Store any leftovers in small containers or jars for future use.

 TIP: This recipe makes 1 paint. You'll need to repeat a total of 4 times to make each color.

Building Block Bath Crayons

What kid doesn't like to build? I sure don't know one. Your kids can now be amazing little architects by drawing up blueprints on the bathroom walls and designing the next skyscraper. All it takes is a few ingredients to make these building block bath crayons that get your kids thinking creatively in more ways than one.

YIELD: About 6 crayons (depending on mold used)

MATERIALS

1½ lb (500 g) white soap base

Essential oil, optional

Red food coloring

Blue food coloring

Yellow food coloring

Green food coloring

Building block silicone mold

DIRECTIONS

1. Cut your melt-and-pour soap into cubes and place into a microwave safe bowl. Do not allow the soap to burn. Heat for 30 seconds in the microwave, stir and repeat until melted before adding the essential oil. For these molds you will need about 1½ pounds (500 g) of soap (can estimate or weigh to be exact).

2. Divide the melted soap equally into 4 small bowls. Color each bowl separately. Start with red and add about 10 to 20 drops of red food coloring to one bowl. Stir well until all the color is mixed into the soap.

3. Repeat the previous step with additional colors. The more food coloring you use, the darker the crayons will be.

4. Pour the mixtures into the cavities of the building block molds and let harden. I usually allow these to harden overnight before removing from the mold.

5. To remove from the mold, gently press from the backside of the mold to release the crayons.

6. Use them immediately or store in an airtight container for future use.

 TIP: Test the bath crayons on a small area of your bathtub or bath walls to ensure the food coloring won't stain. This is typically not an issue, but it may vary depending on the type of material you are applying the crayon to.

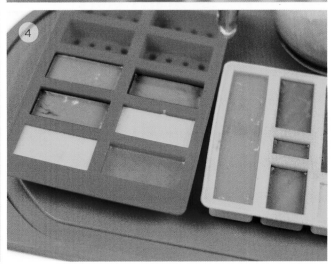

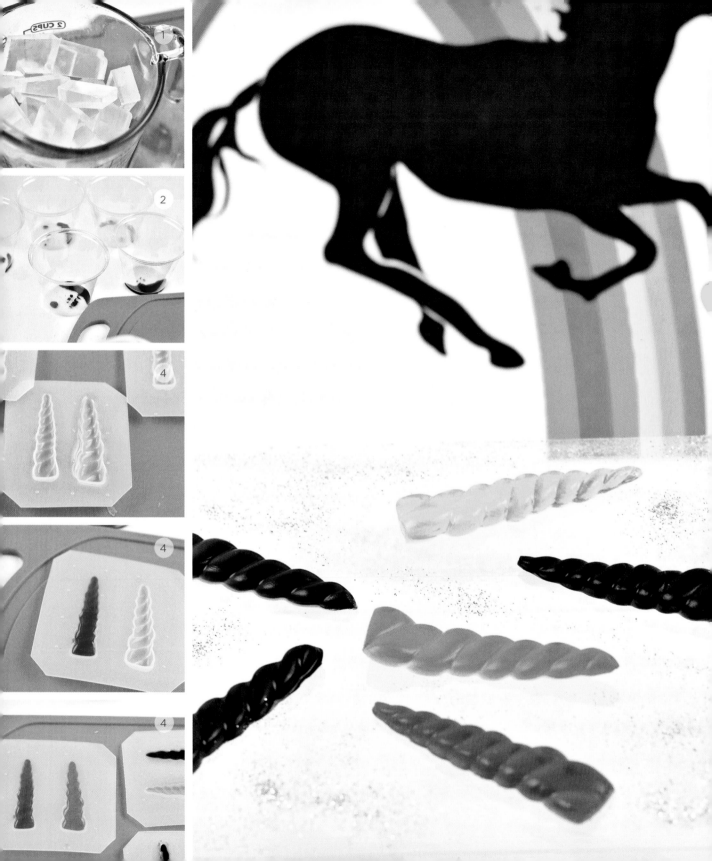

Unicorn Horn Bath Crayons

Everything is better with a unicorn in tow or at least a unicorn horn! This twisted little horn will help you paint dozens of rainbows so your life is always guaranteed to be filled with color and magic.

YIELD: 6 crayons

MATERIALS

1 lb (450 g) clear soap base

4–5 drops bubblegum fragrance oil, optional

1 tbsp (14 g) iridescent super sparkle glitter (skin-safe)

Red food coloring

Blue food coloring

Yellow food coloring

Green food coloring

Neon purple food coloring

Neon pink food coloring

Unicorn horn plastic mold (can be found at an online retailer, such as Etsy)

DIRECTIONS

1. Cut your melt-and-pour soap into cubes and place into a microwave safe bowl. Do not allow the soap to burn. Heat for 30 seconds in the microwave, stir and repeat until melted. Add your fragrance oil and glitter and stir well.

2. Divide the melted soap equally into 6 small bowls. Color each bowl separately. Start with red and add about 10 to 20 drops of red food coloring to one bowl. Stir well until all the color is mixed into the soap.

3. Repeat the previous step with additional colors. The more food coloring you use, the darker the crayons will be.

4. Pour the mixtures into the cavities of the unicorn horn molds and let harden. I usually allow these to harden overnight before removing from the mold.

5. To remove from the mold, gently press from the backside of the mold to release the crayons.

6. Use them immediately or store in an airtight container for future use.

 TIP: Test the bath crayons on a small area of your bathtub or bath walls to ensure the food coloring won't stain. This is typically not an issue, but it may vary depending on the type of material you are applying the crayon to.

Witches' Brew Bath Paints

Double, double toil and trouble! These wicked bath paints will be the perfect pairing with a warm and bubbly brew—I mean, bath! Whip this brew up in no time so your little ghouls can paint their favorite spooky picture!

YIELD: 4 paints

MATERIALS

Shaving cream

Mini plastic cauldrons

Food coloring (in a variety of colors)

Paintbrushes

DIRECTIONS

1. Press the nozzle of your shaving cream and fill each small plastic cauldron to just below the rim.

2. In one of the cauldrons, add a few drops of food coloring. You can even mix colors such as red and yellow to make orange. Repeat this step with additional colors. Think green, purple, blue and orange for authentic witches' brew!

3. Use your paintbrushes (witches' brooms) to stir in each color until the shaving cream is your desired color. Use the paintbrushes to paint all sorts of creepy things onto the walls of your tub!

 TIP: Test the bath paints on a small area of your bathtub or bath walls to ensure the food coloring won't stain. This is typically not an issue, but it may vary depending on the type of material you are applying the bath paints to.

1

2

3

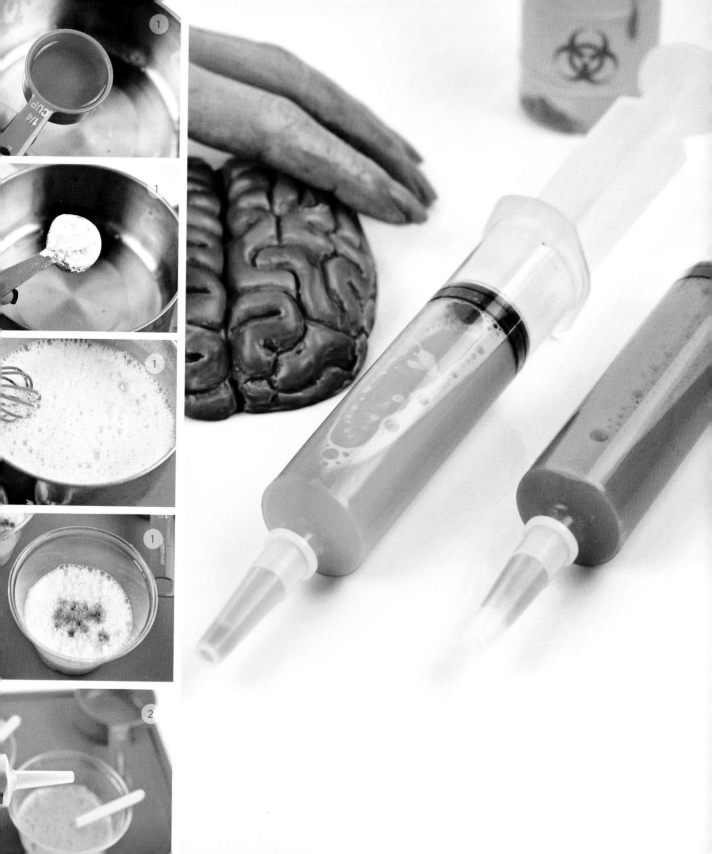

Zombie Virus Bath Paints

An evil corporation has started to bring on the apocalypse. With the outbreak quickly spreading, only you can save the rest of humanity. Have fun disposing the rest of the virus vials down the drain and watch the dreams of the evil corporation shatter. But remember to take extreme precaution to avoid your mouth and eyes as even the smallest amount of exposure can cause you to roam the streets looking for brains too.

YIELD: 2 paints

MATERIALS

½ cup (118 ml) baby shampoo

2 tbsp (1 g) cornstarch

3 tbsp (45 ml) water

Green food coloring

Large syringes (without the needle)

Red food coloring

DIRECTIONS

1. In a bowl, mix the baby shampoo, cornstarch and water. Divide the mixture equally into two plastic cups. Add 3 to 4 drops of green food coloring to the first cup and mix well. If the consistency is too thick, add a bit more water.

2. Use the syringe to draw up the mixture then set aside.

3. Repeat the steps above with the red food coloring and second cup.

4. Once your syringes are filled, quickly dispose of the virus by squirting them in and around the bath.

BEDTIME READINESS

Have you ever wondered how monsters get to sleep at night? The secret is all in the bath! Use a mixture of these soothing bath salts or bubbly bubble baths and you'll want to be tucked right into the covers. Of course, not before checking for monsters under your bed or in your closet!

Butterscotch Brew Bath Salts

Catch your golden sphere full of butterscotch brew bath salts. Does your body ache after broomstick practice? Soak away the blues with a little bit of magic. Any wizard will tell you they are a must!

YIELD: 1 bath salt (depending on the size of your plastic ornament)

MATERIALS

1 cup (225 g) coarse sea salt

2 cups (450 g) Epsom salt

½ cup (113 g) baking soda

1 tsp (5 ml) gold sparkle mica

2–3 drops butterscotch fragrance oil

2–3 drops yellow food coloring

Small funnel

Large round plastic ornament

2 white feathers

Hot glue gun and glue

DIRECTIONS

1. In a bowl, combine the sea salt, Epsom salt, baking soda and mica. Mix well. Add the fragrance oil and food coloring and mix again. You want a light brown/butterscotch color.

2. Use the funnel and a spoon to scoop the bath salts into your plastic ornament then replace the top.

3. Once the ornament is filled, it's time to attach the feathers. Hot glue a feather onto each side of the ornament.

4. After a long day at broomstick practice, grab this and pour some into the bath. You will be amazed at how fabulous these smell!

(continued)

Butterscotch Brew
Bath Salts (cont.)

Laser Sword Bath Salts

Regardless of the side you choose, I think it's safe to say at this point we all have a favorite laser sword color. You will love making these to cut and blast your way through bubbles and to fight off the bad guys. When all is said and done, you can open and dump the colored bath salts into a tub of water and watch the water turn the color of your chosen side.

YIELD: 3 bath salts (depending on the size of your test tubes)

MATERIALS

1 cup (225 g) coarse sea salt

2 cups (450 g) Epsom salt

½ cup (113.4 g) baking soda

2-3 drops lemon essential oil

Red food coloring

Blue food coloring

Green food coloring

Small funnel

Plastic test tubes

Black washi tape or electrical tape

Silver washi tape or duct tape

Red foam sheet

DIRECTIONS

1. In a bowl, combine the sea salt, Epsom salt and baking soda. Mix well. Add the essential oil and mix again.

2. Divide the mixture into 3 separate bowls (if you plan to color the bath salts different colors for the laser swords).

3. In the first bowl, add 5 to 6 drops of red food coloring and stir. Keep stirring until all of the clumps are gone (you can also use your fingers to break up any clumps). If you want a deeper color, add more red food coloring. Repeat this step with the blue and green food coloring.

4. Use the funnel and spoon to scoop the bath salts into a plastic tube. For example, you will place all of the red in 1 tube and all of the green in another tube. These are your "laser swords."

5. The rounded end of the plastic tube will be the top so add the lid to the bottom then turn upside down. Apply the black washi tape over the lid to secure it. This will also become the handle for your laser sword. Use pieces of the silver washi tape to add additional details to the handle. Then cut out a small red circle from the red foam sheet and hot glue it as the bottom of the handle.

6. Gift to friends and family. When ready, remove the tape at the bottom and turn the tube right side up. Dump into a warm bath and enjoy!

(continued)

Genie in a Bottle Bubble Bath

Don't you wish that bath time could be more fun? Wish granted! Just rub this magic lamp and pour the bath potion into the water. Bubbles will emerge making everything more fun. Remember that now you've only got two wishes left, so choose them wisely!

YIELD: 1 bubble bath

MATERIALS

2 cups (500 ml) clear and unscented bubble bath

5–6 drops neon blue food coloring

2–3 drops blueberry fragrance oil

Plastic genie lamp

DIRECTIONS

1. In a bowl, combine the bubble bath, food coloring and fragrance oil. Mix well.

2. Pour the mixture into the plastic genie lamp.

3. When ready to use, give the lamp a little rub and pour some into the tub. Pour under the running water and watch the bubbles come to life!

Mad Scientist Bath Salt Set

Does bath time make you mad? Sounds like a scientific problem. One that can only be solved by making wicked experiments working in the lab late at night. You might just end up giving yourself a nice little fright with the amazing bath salts you create.

YIELD: 3 bath salts (depending on the size of your test tubes)

MATERIALS

1 cup (225 g) coarse sea salt

2 cups (450 g) Epsom salt

½ cup (113 g) baking soda

2-3 drops lemon essential oil

Blue food coloring

Purple food coloring

Orange food coloring

Small funnel

Plastic test tubes (with a stand)

DIRECTIONS

1. In a bowl, combine the sea salt, Epsom salt and baking soda. Mix well. Add the essential oil and mix again.

2. Divide the mixture into 3 separate bowls (if you plan to color the bath salts different colors for the different solutions).

3. In the first bowl, add 5 to 6 drops of blue food coloring and stir. Keep stirring until all of the clumps are gone (you can also use your fingers to break up any clumps). If you want a deeper color, add more blue food coloring. You can totally wear gloves in this step!

4. Repeat the step above with the remaining food colors. Use the funnel and spoon to scoop the bath salts into a plastic tube. For example, you will place all of the blue in 1 tube and all of the orange in another tube. These are your "scientific solutions."

5. Once all of the tubes are filled, place them into the stand and prepare for the most scientific bath you have ever had! Store any leftovers by placing a lid on top and keeping them in a cool and dry place!

Mutant Ooze Bubble Bath

Are bad guys running rampant in your neighborhood? Maybe what you need is some mutant ooze and little reptilian friends to save the day. Just make sure you have pizza ready for when they get home from a long day of fighting crime.

YIELD: 1 bubble bath (depending on the size of your plastic tube)

MATERIALS

2 cups (500 ml) clear and unscented bubble bath

3-4 drops neon green food coloring

1-2 drops yellow food coloring

2-3 drops lemon essential oil

2-3 drops lime essential oil

Plastic tube container

4 small plastic turtle toys

DIRECTIONS

1. In a bowl, combine the bubble bath, food coloring and essential oils. Mix well.

2. Pour half of the mixture into the plastic tube container then add your little turtle toys. Pour the remaining mixture into the tube.

3. When ready to use, just pour some of this ooze into your bath and watch the bubbles emerge from the water much like a turtle comes out of his shell!

Poisonous Potion Bubble Bath

Boys and girls of every age, would you like to see something strange? Jump into the bath and you will see, a bubbly bath that will get you clean. This is a bubble bath but not just any bubble bath; it is a poisonous potion that fills your bath with fright.

YIELD: 3 bubble baths

MATERIALS

3 cups (750 ml) clear and unscented bubble bath, divided

4–5 drops neon green food coloring

Lime essential oil (for the green)

1–2 drops red food coloring

2–3 drops yellow food coloring

Orange essential oil (for the orange)

3–4 drops neon purple food coloring

Lavender essential oil (for the purple)

3 plastic bottles (different shapes and sizes to look like potions)

DIRECTIONS

1. In a bowl, combine 1 cup (240 ml) of the bubble bath, neon green food coloring and the lime essential oil. Set aside.

2. Next, combine 1 cup (240 ml) of the bubble bath, red food coloring, yellow food coloring and the orange essential oil. Set aside.

3. In the last bowl, combine 1 cup (240 ml) of the bubble bath, neon purple food coloring and the lavender essential oil. Set aside.

4. Pour each mixture into one of the plastic bottles you have so you end up with one orange colored bubble bath, one green and one purple.

5. When ready to bathe, just run some of this potion under the warm water. A certain ragdoll would be so proud of the bubbliness you have accomplished.

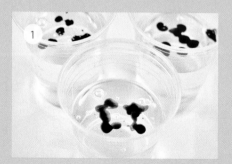

Wizard Staff Bubble Bath

What does every wizard need (besides an epic beard of course)? A book full of spells and a magical staff filled with bubble bath to keep all those trolls and sirens away! With this staff, you'll be on your way to mastering wizardry.

YIELD: 1 bubble bath (depending on the size of your test tube)

MATERIALS

2 cups (500 ml) clear and unscented bubble bath

3-4 drops orange food coloring

3-4 drops orange essential oil

1 tsp (5 g) iridescent super sparkle glitter (skin-safe)

Long clear plastic test tube container (with a flat lid on top)

Hot glue gun and glue

Medium marble

Milk chocolate brown glue gun sticks

DIRECTIONS

1. In a bowl, combine the bubble bath, food coloring, essential oil and glitter. Mix well. Pour the bubble bath mixture into your test tube container and place the lid on top.

2. Hot glue the marble to the lid of the container (this is the top of your staff). Now use the brown glue gun sticks and wrap glue around the outside of your staff (the orange bubble bath will peak through) and the brown will look like branches wrapped around the staff.

3. Once the glue has time to dry, it's time for some wizardry! Just open, pour and watch the bubbles appear like some sort of sorcery is involved.

Robot Food Bubble Bath

Want to unwind and gear down for the night? Dump a load of this robot food into the bath and you'll be on your way to recharging and activating functional levels in no time. Don't worry, you won't get rusty when wet!

YIELD: 1 bubble bath

MATERIALS

2 cups (500 ml) clear and unscented bubble bath

2 tbsp (23 g) sterling silver mica powder

3–4 drops energy fragrance oil

Large plastic container

Hot glue gun and glue

Small metal gears

DIRECTIONS

1. In a bowl, combine the bubble bath, silver mica and fragrance oil. Mix well. Pour the bubble bath mixture into your container and place the lid on top.

2. Hot glue the tiny metal gears onto the lid and front of the container.

3. When you feel the need to refuel on energy, hop into the bath and pour some of this into the water. Your gears will feel nice and lubricated and you will have a recharged battery!

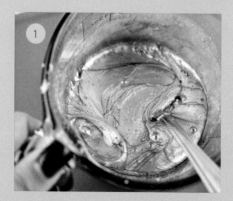

AFTER BATH CARE

After the apocalypse has come and gone, the only thing left to do is rebuild. Start by applying lotions and balms to soften the wounds acquired from being chased by zombies. Don't worry about the scents, as we even have a way to mask your smell in case the virus returns.

Boogie Man Lotion

You're joking—you're joking—I can't believe my eyes! This lotion is so intense and spooky you may just want to cry! This lotion will leave you feeling oogey, boogey soft but beware, there may just be bugs inside!

YIELD: 1 lotion

MATERIALS

2 cups (450 ml) unscented white lotion base

4-5 drops neon green food coloring

2-3 drops lime essential oil

Mini toy bugs (think mini ants, mini glow in the dark maggots, etc.)

Plastic bottle (look for one with a cylinder triangle-type shape)

Black marker

Hot glue gun and glue

2 small dice

DIRECTIONS

1. In a bowl, combine the lotion base, food coloring and essential oil. Mix well using a hand mixer.

2. Next, add your bugs into the bowl but gently fold them in using a spoon (the hand mixer might break them).

3. Fill your bottle with your lotion mixture until full. Once filled, take a black marker and draw on the boogie monster's face (2 slanted slots for the eyes and a slanted mouth).

4. Hot glue 2 small dice to the top of the soap pump and make sure they are pointed on snake eyes!

5. Use this lotion whenever you feel a little itch coming on!

Eyeball Lip Balm

Look into my eye and you will see, a solution for lips of sorrow that have no view of another tomorrow. A little goes a long way in helping those lips be ready for kissing frogs and becoming the queen you were meant to be.

YIELD: 1 lip balm (depending on the size of your lip balm container)

MATERIALS

2 tbsp (30 ml) coconut oil

2 tbsp (28 g) shea butter

2 tbsp (28 g) white beeswax pellets

1 drop lemon essential oil, optional

⅛ tsp activated charcoal

⅛ tsp blue mica

Plastic pipette

Round metal lip balm containers

DIRECTIONS

1. In a saucepan, add the coconut oil, shea butter and beeswax pellets. Heat over medium heat until they melt. Stirring during this step helps. Remove from the heat when melted. Add the essential oil (if using) and mix again.

2. Divide the mixture into 3 separate bowls (equal amount in each). In the first bowl, add the activated charcoal and stir. It should make this a nice black color which will be used for the pupil of the eye.

3. In the second bowl, add the blue mica; this will be the iris of the eye. Use your plastic pipette to fill your lip balm container with the white melted oils (the base of the eye). Allow this to harden.

4. Next, add a small amount of the blue-colored mixture on top (creating a small circle, being careful not to cover all of the white part). Allow this to harden. Repeat the last step with the black-colored mixture, but the circle should be smaller and on top of the blue part. Allow all of the mixture to harden entirely.

5. When ready, rub your finger into the eye and apply to your lips!

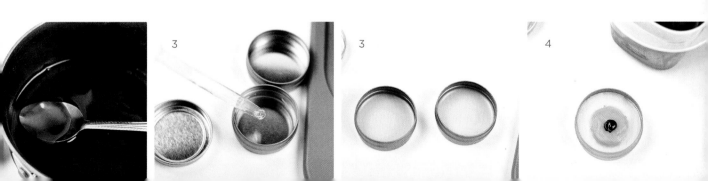

Ice Queen Lotion Bars

Let it go—let it go—let the itchy and flaky skin move along. These lotion bars are made of magically snowy powers, but don't worry, the cold won't bother you anyway. Just keep them away from the sun, or you'll find out what happens to icy solids when they get warm.

YIELD: 6 lotion bars

MATERIALS

2 cups (473 ml) coconut oil

2 cups (435 g) white beeswax pellets

Essential oil

1 tsp (5 g) iridescent super sparkle glitter (skin-safe)

1 tsp (5 g) blue mica colorant

Snowflake silicone mold

DIRECTIONS

1. In a saucepan, add the coconut oil and beeswax pellets. Heat over medium heat until they melt. Stirring during this step helps. Once melted, remove from heat and stir in your essential oil and glitter.

2. Pour the mixture into 2 separate bowls (equal amount in each). One bowl you will leave white and the other bowl you will add your blue mica colorant and stir well.

3. Take the uncolored mixture and pour it into a cavity of the mold. Continue this step until the mixture is gone. Repeat this step using the blue colored mixture.

4. Allow these to cool and harden (may take several hours).

5. Once hardened, you can remove from the molds and use them right away. Rub them on your skin until it's nice and warm then it works just like lotion! Something only an ice queen could appreciate!

Radioactive Lotion

Warning: This lotion may cause intense fevers, blood shot eyes, glowing yellow skin and hunger for brains. Proceed with caution. If a burning sensation for the eating of flesh occurs, visit your nearby CDC emergency tent for treatment and further instruction.

YIELD: 1 lotion

MATERIALS

1 cup (225 g) basic lotion base (unscented and uncolored lotion)

3-4 drops lemon essential oil

1 tbsp (15 ml) yellow baby duck mica powder

Plastic container with lid

Paper

Black permanent marker

Tape

DIRECTIONS

1. Place your lotion base into a microwave safe bowl and heat for 30 seconds. Remove and stir. Complete this process until the lotion base is melted.

2. Add the essential oil and the mica powder to the mixture and stir well. If you feel your lotion is too light, you can add 1 teaspoon at a time until you get a nice yellow color. Just be careful not to add too much or it may cause staining.

3. Carefully pour the melted mixture into your plastic container and allow it to cool down to room temperature. It will then be a solid again.

4. Place the lid onto the top of your container. On a piece of paper, draw out the radioactive symbol. Cut the symbol out then tape it to the front of your container to give it that authentic radioactive look.

5. When ready, apply the radioactive lotion to your skin and watch as your skin gets nice and moisturized!

 TIP: You can also print out the symbol on your computer then cut and apply it to the front of your container.

ZOMBIE REPELLENT

Zombie Repellent Spray

Zombies are beginning to adapt and their sense of smell is changing.
The only way to mask your scent is to use this repellent spray. A few bursts of this and
you can walk amongst the dead without them even noticing you.

YIELD: 1 spray

MATERIALS

1 cup (250 ml) distilled water

1 tbsp (15 ml) witch hazel

3–4 drops lime essential oil

1–2 drops neon green food coloring

Spray bottle

White paper

Black permanent marker

Transparent tape

DIRECTIONS

1. In a bowl, combine the distilled water, witch hazel, essential oil and food coloring. Mix well. Carefully pour the mixture into a spray bottle.

2. Take your white piece of paper and cut a small strip off that will fit onto the front of the bottle. Using your black marker write, "Zombie Repellent" on the paper and then tape it to the front of your spray bottle.

3. When you know you'll be around those zombies, just spray a few small bursts on your body. You'll smell like limes, and zombies hate limes, so they'll stay away!

 TIP: You can also print out a biohazard symbol to cut and tape onto the front of your bottle. Have fun with your newfound spray!

Acknowledgments

With a house full of nerds, you can imagine our lives are far from boring. From the collectible-filled shelves to the voices of YouTubers echoing through the halls, our home is an abundant supply of nerdy inspiration. But none of that can amount to the amazing people that helped turn this book from a dream to a reality.

First, I want to thank my wonderfully nerdy, gamer husband who worked side-by-side with me for many sleepless nights. He knew exactly how to turn my creatively insane ideas into a reality and was so supportive through this entire journey. I love you to the moon and back.

Next, I want to thank my boys. Kayzen, you wonderfully little nerdy human you, your silliness and extreme knowledge on video games never ceases to amaze me. You've taught me strategy and the perfect way to keep the creepers away. I couldn't have done this without you! My dear sweet, Tarek, you don't even know it yet but you were a huge inspiration in the making of this book. Your quiet yet mischievous attitude taught me to be fearless and just go for it. I love watching you grow and cannot wait to see the perfect little nerd we know you will become.

I also want to give a big thanks to my guest writers. First, to Jamie Harrington, who is a dear friend and mentor of mine, who supported me along the way. She told me what I needed to hear even when it wasn't what I wanted to hear. Our love for all things nerdy is what brought us together and I am forever grateful for her friendship. Next, Holly Homer who is also a dear friend that mentored me and showed me anything is possible as long as you want it bad enough. She is brilliant in everything she does and I only hope to have half of the amount of her wisdom one day.

A big thanks to the rest of my family and friends who supported me and helped me get the words out when my mind was drawing a blank. Each and every one of you were so supportive and believed in me even when I didn't believe in myself. You know who you are and you are all amazing!

Last but certainly not least, I want to thank Page Street Publishing for giving me this amazing opportunity. The entire team, including Elizabeth and Will, rolled with my ideas and were so patient when I asked a million questions. I am forever grateful for the opportunity they have given me and I could not be more excited to show this book to the world!

About the Author

Brittanie Pyper has been blogging at Simplistically Living for over four years. She started as a deal blogger but knew her heart really lay within the creativity of crafts. With her kingdom of hearts by her side and a full health bar of gold, this geek goddess knew anything was possible. Her love for video games and all things geeky did not go unnoticed and it quickly turned into a full-time gig. She now spends her time raising the next generation of geeks and teaching them all that she knows. When she isn't teaching, writing or crafting, you will find her with a gaming controller in hand and coffee by her side. All while sporting unicorn slippers. Because unicorns are awesome!

You can geek out with Brittanie at:

HER BLOG: http://www.simplisticallyliving.com/

FACEBOOK: https://www.facebook.com/SimplisticallyLiving

INSTAGRAM: https://www.instagram.com/simplisticallyliving/

PINTEREST: https://www.pinterest.com/simplistcliving/

TWITTER: https://twitter.com/simplistcliving

Index

As a member of 1% for the Planet, Page Street Publishing protects our planet by donating to nonprofits like The Trustees, which focuses on local land conservation. Learn more at onepercentfortheplanet.org.